PIONEERS OF SCIENCE

ALEXANDER FLEMING

Paul Bennett

Wayland

Pioneers of Science

Archimedes
Alexander Graham Bell
Karl Benz
Marie Curie
Thomas Edison
Albert Einstein
Michael Faraday
Alexander Fleming
Galileo
Edward Jenner
Joseph Lister
Guglielmo Marconi
Isaac Newton
Louis Pasteur
Leonardo da Vinci
James Watt

Series and book editor Rosemary Ashley
Designer David Armitage

First published in 1992 by
Wayland (Publishers) Ltd
61 Western Road, Hove
East Sussex BN3 1JD, England

British Library Cataloguing in Publication Data
Bennett, Paul
   Alexander Fleming. – (Pioneers of science)
   I. Title   II. Series
   616.014092

   ISBN 0–7502–0320–X

Typeset by DP Press Ltd, Sevenoaks, Kent
Printed in Italy by Rotolito Lombarda S.p.A.
Bound in France by A.G.M.

Contents

1 The Fleming Myth

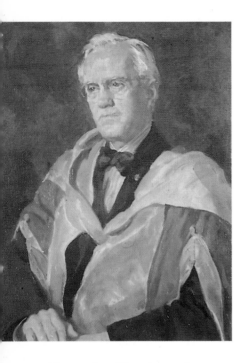

Alexander Fleming – the discoverer of the life-saving drug, penicillin.

Throughout history, huge numbers of people have fallen victim to killer diseases. Some of these diseases are caused by bacteria – tiny organisms that can be seen under a microscope. Most treatments were not very effective and so even minor infections were feared, as cancer and AIDS are today.

Just fifty years ago, hospital wards were full of patients with septic infections – infections where disease-causing bacteria destroy body tissues and cause very serious illness. For example, pneumonia was once a very common and dangerous disease of the lungs that could affect both young and old alike. The bacteria caused inflammation of the lungs, and the air sacs in the lungs filled up with pus. As the disease got worse, the patient would cough, suffer pain and find it increasingly difficult to breathe. Often pus would form in the chest as well as the lungs, and the patient would need a tube inserted into the chest to drain out the pus. This treatment often went on for weeks until the patient either recovered or died, depending on the severity of the illness.

Early in the Second World War (1939–45), a 'wonder drug' was widely publicized in Britain. Called penicillin, the public learnt that it would cure all sorts of infections, from simple abscesses or pneumonia to the dreaded gas gangrene, which often affected soldiers wounded in battle. Understandably, the news that a life-saving drug had been discovered was greeted with much excitement by the general public, and there were calls that the government should find the resources to start mass-producing the drug in

Britain at once. By 1943, penicillin had become a vital part of the war effort, curing many wounded servicemen of their infections, and allowing them to return to active duty.

The man who discovered this miracle cure, Alexander Fleming, quickly became a national hero and is widely accepted as a great scientist.

French nurses care for a soldier wounded in battle during the First World War (1914–18). Before the development of antibiotics, even a minor scratch could lead to a life-threatening infection.

Bacteria – friend or foe?

Bacteria are tiny organisms (micro-organisms) that can be seen under a microscope. Bacteria and other minute living things that cause disease are often called germs. Bacteria are responsible for the killer diseases tuberculosis, tetanus and legionnaire's disease, and are a cause of food poisoning. However, not all bacteria are harmful and some are extremely useful to us. For example, the making of yoghurt and cheese are dependent on these tiny organisms, and bacteria, in the form of yeast, are used to make bread rise and turn the sugar in wine and beer into alcohol. This false-colour, highly magnified picture shows that many thousands can fit on a pin-head.

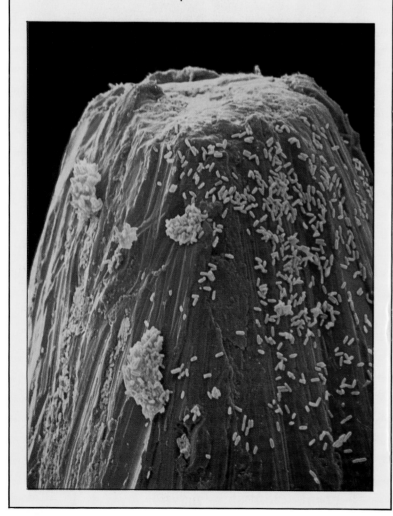

Howard Florey (centre, front row) and his team at the Sir William Dunn School of Pathology at Oxford University. Florey and his colleagues developed penicillin into an effective treatment for infections.

Fleming discovered penicillin by accident, and it was the first antibiotic drug for the treatment of infections. The development of antibiotics is seen as perhaps the greatest contribution to medical treatment this century, and so it is not surprising that Fleming has received many tributes. Because of his discovery he became a legend in his own lifetime, and is regarded as a key figure in the saving of lives.

But although it was Fleming who discovered penicillin, it was a team of biochemists, led by Howard Florey, who developed it into a drug that doctors could use. Without their crucial work, it is possible that the life-saving potential of penicillin would never have been realized.

2 The Young Alec

Alexander Fleming was born on 6 August 1881, at Lochfield Farm in Ayrshire, Scotland. His father was a hill farmer who, by his two marriages, had eight children. Alec, as he was known, was the second youngest.

The secluded farm – the nearest neighbours were two km away – provided just enough income to keep the large Fleming family clothed and fed. Alec was still very young when his father died and his mother, Grace, was left to run the farm. All the children helped as best they could until they were old enough to earn their living away from home.

Although the farm provided only a poor income, it did give a healthy way of life that suited young Alec. He was a very active child and enjoyed exploring the surrounding moor and hills, and would spend hours stalking animals, fishing and examining plants.

Lochfield farm, Alec's birthplace. The number of farm buildings has increased since Alec lived there as a boy.

Fleming is photographed visiting the school house at Loudoun Moor. As a boy he attended this school before going to the school at Darvel.

When he was ten, Alec attended a school in a nearby town, Darvel. He walked the six km from the farm to school in all weathers. Alec liked school and developed a love of sports that was to last throughout his life and was later to play an important part in determining his career. During a playground incident, he broke his nose, an accident which gave him his very distinctive profile – he looked as if he had been a boxer all his life! When he was twelve, Alec went to the Academy at Kilmarnock for eighteen months, to continue his schooling. Then, at the age of fourteen, he travelled south to London to stay with one of his brothers, Tom, who had qualified as a doctor.

For the next two years, Alec attended the Polytechnic School in London's Regent Street. When he completed his schooling, in 1897, he found a job with a shipping company. His work as a clerk was very dull and, in 1900, when there was a call for volunteers for the army, he joined the London Scottish Regiment as a part-time soldier. The Boer War (1899–1902) had begun the year before in South Africa, between Britain and the Dutch settlers there, and young men were needed by the British Army. Alec never saw action in this war, but the regiment gave him a chance to play sports with other young Scotsmen.

During the course of his training, Alec discovered that he was a very good shot with a rifle. He remained with the London Scottish as a part-time soldier for fourteen years, and helped the rifle team to carry off the celebrated *Daily Telegraph* Cup in June 1908.

In 1901, one of his uncles died and left Alec £250. This gave the young man the chance to leave his boring office job and go to medical school to become a doctor like his brother, Tom. As Alec had no university diploma, he had first to pass a scholarship examination. In July 1901, he entered the University of London Scholarship in Natural Sciences, and he passed with the best marks of all those who entered. This meant that he could choose which of the twelve London medical schools to attend. He chose to go to St Mary's Hospital, Paddington, not because of its excellence, but because he once enjoyed playing water polo against them for the London Scottish!

Opposite *The front page of the June 1908 issue of the* London Scottish Regimental Gazette *shows Alec (front row left) as part of the rifle team that won the* Daily Telegraph *Cup.*

THE LONDON SCOTTISH REGIMENTAL GAZETTE

No. 150.—Vol. XIII.]   JUNE, 1908.   (Price 4d. Annual Subscription, 3s.) Post free.) [Entered at Stationers Hall

"DAILY TELEGRAPH" CUP TEAM.

Photo Keenes & Co.]   **MARCHING TO VICTORY.**   [Woking.

From Student to Research Assistant

At St Mary's Hospital, Fleming quickly established himself as a brilliant medical student and consistently reached the top of his class. He was several years older than most of his fellow students, many of whom had come to St Mary's straight from school. Fleming believed that this gave him an advantage over them as he had more experience of life, which allowed him to complete his studies with confidence. He worked hard at his studies, helped by his eye for detail and a very good memory. He found the work easy and had plenty of time for his favourite sports – including

St Mary's Hospital, Paddington. Fleming's laboratory was at the front of the building on the third floor at the right-hand corner.

Fleming attending a lecture at St Mary's (fourth from the right in the front row).

shooting. In 1906, Fleming passed his examinations with honours and qualified as a doctor. At that time he intended to become a surgeon and the year before had taken the first examinations for the Royal College of Surgeons. However, it was by no means certain that Fleming would be able to become a surgeon at St Mary's. He needed to pay the fees for taking further medical qualifications, including the second part of the examination for the Royal College of Surgeons. Vacancies were few and far between, so what would he do now? For a second time, he would allow his interest in sport to determine the course he would take.

Almoth Wright (1861–1947) the head of the inoculation department at St Mary's. He joined the hospital in 1902 and Fleming became a member of his department in 1906.

One of the members of the teaching staff at St Mary's was Almoth Wright, the head of the inoculation department. A member of his department, a doctor called John Freeman, wanted Fleming to stay at St Mary's to strengthen his rifle team. Using his powers of persuasion, he won Fleming over to the idea that he should work in the inoculation department, which would earn him the money he needed to take further examinations. Wright was keen to build a team of able young researchers and, as Freeman pointed out, Fleming's powers of observation, skill with his hands and scientific mind would make him an ideal research assistant. Consequently, Fleming was invited by Wright to join the department, and he accepted.

Wright was a bacteriologist and he believed that immunization was the key to the treatment of infectious diseases. Immunization is a method of protecting a person against a particular infection. This involves introducing a substance into the body by inoculation – a method used by an Englishman, Edward Jenner (1749–1823), to give a person the disease cowpox. Jenner discovered that if a person caught this disease, it would make them immune to the dreaded disease, smallpox. Smallpox killed between a quarter and a half of those who caught it, and left those who survived the disease terribly scarred and often with serious side effects, such as brain damage and deafness. In Jenner's time no one knew the cause of diseases and infections, and it was not until 1861 that the French bacteriologist Louis Pasteur (1822–95) established that micro-organisms were the cause of disease.

Fleming at his bench in the inoculation department. The photograph was taken in about 1909.

Louis Pasteur

A Dutch naturalist, Antoni van Leeuwenhoek (1632–1723), had observed minute organisms under his simple microscope, but the cause of diseases remained a mystery until the second half of the nineteenth century. From the mid-1860s, the Frenchman, Pasteur, carried out a series of experiments and established that diseases were caused by micro-organisms. Pasteur's research into the process of fermentation and into animal diseases, such as fowl cholera and anthrax, laid the foundations of modern bacteriology. He also produced a vaccine for the killer disease, rabies, which was used successfully on a nine-year-old boy who had caught the disease.

Wright was very interested in the way the human body destroys the bacteria that cause disease. By being inoculated, the body 'learns' to kill the organism, so that if the same organism is encountered again, a rapid and effective defence is mobilized. Wright also thought that it was possible to cure a disease by giving a vaccine, which would help the body's natural defences to fight infections.

Fleming's work in the inoculation department involved taking a specimen (a sample of blood or saliva, for example) from an infected person, and putting it into a Petri dish or plate (a shallow, circular dish with a cover, made of clear glass or, today, plastic). The dish contained a medium – food for the bacteria in the specimen. The medium and Petri dish provided ideal conditions in which the bacteria could grow. Fleming would then examine the result, or culture, under a microscope to identify the organism that caused the infection.

At first, Fleming saw his job at the inoculation department as a temporary position. In 1908 he took his final examinations, achieving honours in five subjects, and won the University of London

Paul Ehrlich (1854–1915), the German chemist who discovered a cure for the disease, syphilis. The preparation was called 606, and Fleming used it to treat his private patients.

A cartoon of Fleming entitled 'Private 606'. When it was drawn in 1911, Fleming was still a private in the London Scottish Regiment.

Gold Medal for his excellent performance. Later, he also took the second part of the Royal College of Surgeons examination – he now had the opportunity to practise as a fully qualified surgeon, but decided not to do so. He enjoyed the work at the inoculation department; bacteriology, he decided, was his full-time career and, indeed, he spent the next forty-seven years in the department.

In 1909, a German chemist, Paul Ehrlich, finally discovered a cure for the disease syphilis. After six hundred and five failures his next attempt was a success, and so his preparation was nicknamed '606'. Ehrlich's cure involved injecting a chemical into the infected person, which singled out the harmful bacteria and killed them without harming the body's own cells – described by Fleming as a 'magic bullet'. Ehrlich sent some 606 to Wright, who passed it on to Fleming. Wright was scornful of chemical treatments, believing their usefulness was limited.

By now, Fleming had established a private practice – after a full day's work he would give medical treatment to those who did not want to see their local doctor or visit a hospital. The fees from these patients helped to enlarge his own modest income from the inoculation department. Fleming had devised an improved method of diagnosing syphilis, and began to treat sufferers with 606. He earned the nickname 'Private 606', and soon had quite a large practice.

The success of 606 did not impress Wright, who still believed that immunization was the key to the treatment of infectious diseases. Under the influence of Wright and, later, through his experience of treating wounded soldiers during the First World War (1914–18), Fleming grew to doubt the use of chemicals in the treatment of diseases.

When the First World War broke out in August 1914, Fleming accompanied Wright to a research laboratory set up at a casino in Boulogne, France, which had been converted into a hospital. Fleming was no longer a volunteer private in the London Scottish Regiment, he was now a lieutenant in the Royal Army Medical Corps.

Doctors knew that the outcome of the war would be as much decided by the effect of diseases as by battle casualties. Diseases such as typhoid killed so many soldiers during the Boer War that the War Office agreed that British troops should be inoculated with a typhoid vaccine that Wright had developed. Bacteria were also the cause of infections which were killing the wounded in huge numbers. Perhaps as many as one in ten of all deaths were due to gas gangrene and tetanus, and so Wright and his team at the casino hospital began a special study of war wounds.

A false-colour picture of the bacteria that causes the deadly disease, tetanus.

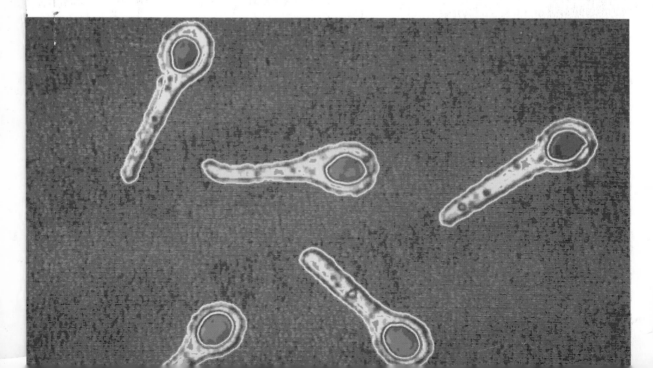

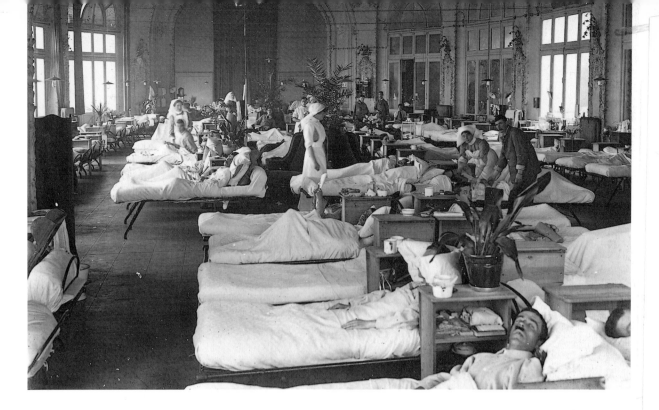

A ward for wounded soldiers at the casino hospital in Boulogne, France. The casino also housed Almoth Wright's team of bacteriologists.

Most battle casualties were infected when they arrived at the hospital. Gas gangrene was particularly feared, as it caused death and decay to tissue and spread very rapidly from the site of the wound. Unless the surgeon could amputate (remove) a leg or arm above the infection, the result was sure to be fatal.

To prevent infections developing, doctors believed that certain chemicals, called antiseptics, would, when applied to wounds, destroy or inhibit the growth of disease-causing bacteria. But during a series of experiments, Fleming discovered that antiseptics actually did more harm than good. They destroyed the patient's own disease-fighting cells more easily than they killed the invading bacteria. Unfortunately, many doctors found this difficult to believe and continued to use antiseptics to treat the wounded.

On 23 December 1915, while on leave in England, Fleming married Sally McElroy, an Irish nurse who ran her own nursing home. Their marriage was to be a long and happy one, and they had a son, Robert, who was born in 1924.

After the war, Wright's group of bacteriologists returned to St Mary's. Fleming was appointed lecturer in bacteriology and in 1921 became assistant director of the inoculation department, which had been renamed Department of Pathology and Research.

In 1922, Fleming made another discovery. During the winter, when he had a cold, some mucus dripped from his nose on to the culture plate that he was examining. Fleming was an untidy worker and liked to keep his cultures for several weeks before discarding them. Consequently, his work bench could become extremely cluttered, but before he had the plates cleaned, he would examine each one to see if anything interesting or unusual had developed.

On the plate that had been splashed by the mucus some weeks earlier, he noticed that areas of the bacteria had not grown – instead of being opaque (cloudy) there were areas which had become clear and lifeless in appearance. His curiosity aroused, Fleming tested samples of mucus from other people to see if the same thing occurred. He found that it did. He then tried tears. Using a squirt of lemon juice he would collect the tears of laboratory workers – for submitting to this ordeal, they would be paid threepence a squirt! The result was the same. In a series of experiments, Fleming went on to prove that many

The shape of bacteria

Bacteria come in all shapes and forms. Most bacteria consist of just one cell which may be spherical or ball-shaped, rod-like, shaped like a spiral, comma shaped or corkscrew shaped. Some bacteria have one or more fine hairs arising from their surface that they use to help them move through watery surroundings. The cell wall is often coated in a slimy substance. Many antibiotics act by destroying this cell wall. Inside the cell is a jelly-like substance that surrounds the nucleus – the compartment that contains material that controls the characteristics and growth of the cell. Some cells that cause disease release a substance that is highly poisonous. Other cells contain a poison that is harmful to the cells of the body, and which is released only when the bacterial cell breaks down or dies and disintegrates.

This rod-shaped bacterium has many fine hairs which help it to move.

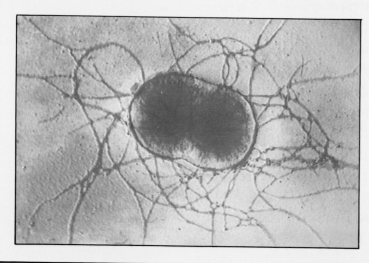

This cartoon pokes fun at Fleming's discovery of lysozyme, the antiseptic found in tears and other body fluids.

body fluids contain a substance that can 'dissolve' certain bacteria with surprising speed.

At Wright's suggestion, the substance was named lysozyme, from the words 'lysing' (which means dissolving), and 'enzyme' (which is a substance essential for the normal functioning and development of the body).

At first, Fleming thought that this chance discovery was of potential significance. Unlike chemical antiseptics, it could kill some bacteria without harming human cells – it was part of the body's own natural defences and so was safe to use.

Assisted by his lifelong friend V.D. Allison, Fleming researched the properties of lysozyme and together they published a paper on the substance. Unfortunately, Fleming's colleagues believed it was an interesting discovery, but not a significant one: lysozyme did not kill disease-causing bacteria and so had no practical value. It has been used in research into bacteria and for treating some eye infections, but no important use has been found for lysozyme in the treatment of life-threatening diseases.

Fleming examining a culture plate. His discovery of penicillin happened by pure chance.

During the First World War, Fleming became convinced that chemicals were not the answer to treating diseases. Ehrlich's 606 had worked on syphilis, but this was an exception to the rule. He believed there must be an agent – a substance that exerts an influence – that could fight bacteria without causing damage to the body's own cells. Lysozyme proved not to be the 'magic bullet' he was looking for as its action was limited.

Six years after discovering lysozyme, Fleming made his most important discovery. One day in September 1928, he started going through some old culture plates. He had just returned from a holiday and, finding nothing of interest, dumped the plates in a disinfectant tray ready for washing up. Luckily, not all the plates were in the disinfectant and when a former colleague called by to see what he had been doing, Fleming showed the visitor some of the plates on top of the pile that had not been spoilt.

Then something caught Fleming's eye. He noticed that one of the plates had gone mouldy, and around the patch of green mould the disease-causing bacteria he had been growing were dying. Where did the mould come from and what was it? Fleming was used to 'things falling out of the air' and spoiling his culture plates. However, the mould was quite a rare one, and it was unlikely that its spores blew in through the window. The spores may have drifted up the staircase from the floor below, where rare types of mould were being collected by a researcher in another department.

Fleming grew a portion of the mould and proved that the 'juice' that the mould produced worked perfectly against many disease-causing bacteria while being harmless to human cells. The mould was identified as *Penicillium notatum*, and Fleming named the substance that it gave off penicillin.

Fleming's desk as it was in 1928 when he discovered penicillin.

This picture shows the original plate on which the Penicillium *mould was discovered (right). Over the years it has deteriorated, and the plate on the left shows how it would have looked in 1928.*

This appeared to be the answer that Fleming had been looking for. But there was a problem. Fleming did not know how to purify the substance enough to use it in injections. A biochemist – someone who studies the chemicals and reactions occurring in an organism – might be able to do this, but there was no one at St Mary's at that time who could help him. Fleming did publish his findings in June 1929, in *The British Journal of Experimental Pathology*. However, its title was rather vague and Fleming was not a good communicator, and so he failed to excite scientists at the time of his discovery. He had a substance which, like lysozyme, could not be used by doctors, and for ten years the revolutionary potential of penicillin went unnoticed.

However, during the next few years one person took up Fleming's challenge. Between 1930 and 1932, Harold Raistrick, a professor at the London School of Hygiene and Tropical Medicine, worked on the mould. He tried to obtain penicillin in a pure form but he only had a limited success – penicillin was very unstable, and when it was extracted from the culture much of it was destroyed.

During the 1930s, Fleming's time was taken up by routine duties at St Mary's. In 1928 he had been made a professor of bacteriology, and spent much of his time testing the vaccines that his department produced.

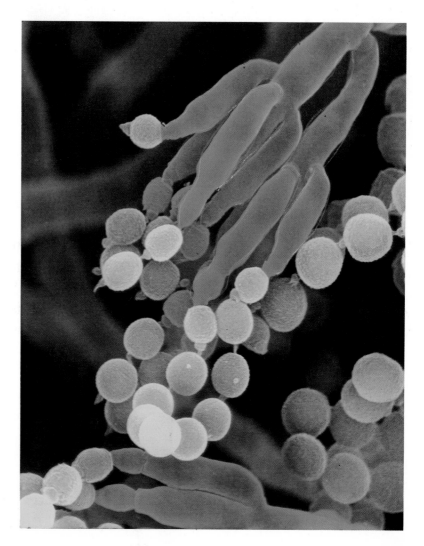

A false-colour, highly magnified picture of the Penicillium *mould releasing its spores.*

The *Penicillium* mould

The antibiotic, penicillin, is derived from the mould *Penicillium notatum*. This close-up picture shows the mould growing in a culture plate. Moulds are a type of fungus that commonly forms a rough, furry coating on decaying material. Some types of *Penicillium* mould grow on decaying food, and some are harmful to humans, causing diseases of the skin and the tissues of the nose and lungs.

Penicillin is usually given by injection to a person with an infection, but is often taken by mouth to treat dental abscesses (a collection of pus around an infected tooth). There are very few unwanted effects. However, there are people who are sensitive to penicillin and develop such reactions as skin rashes, swelling of the throat and fever.

A close-up picture of the fungus, Penicillium notatum, *growing in a culture plate.*

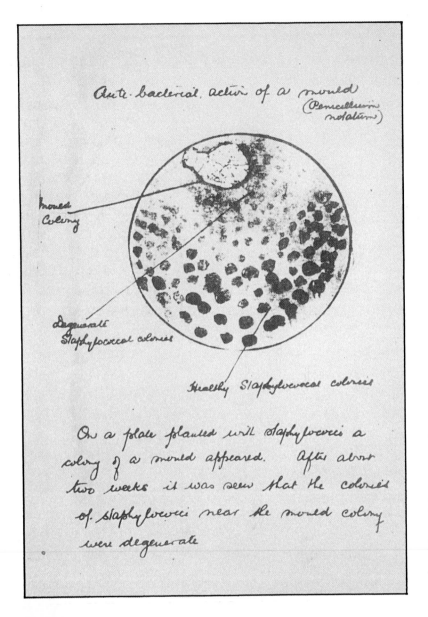

Fleming's bench notes desribing the original culture plate of the Penicillium *mould.*

In 1935, a new treatment for bacterial infections was discovered. Drugs called sulphonamides had been developed, which prevented the growth of bacteria in the body – the body's own natural defences had to kill off the invading organisms. These drugs could be taken by mouth and could be used against a variety of infections. Their effectiveness focused the attention of the medical profession on the treatment of diseases by the use of chemical substances, and gave the stimulus for the difficult task of concentrating penicillin.

The Problem is Solved

At Oxford University, an Australian professor, Howard Florey, had assembled a team of people to work on substances that might be used to treat infections. One of the leaders of his team was Ernst Chain, a refugee who had fled from Nazi Germany in 1933. Chain was a biochemist whose work involved the investigation of anti-bacterial substances. During the late 1930s, Chain searched through over 200 research papers and eventually came across Fleming's ten-year-old report on penicillin. Luckily, Florey's department already

Above *Ernst Chain, a brilliant biochemist and a key member of Florey's team.*

Left *Howard Florey injecting a mouse with penicillin. The experiments carried out on small animals were so successful that the Florey team immediately looked for ways of increasing the production of penicillin for the war effort.*

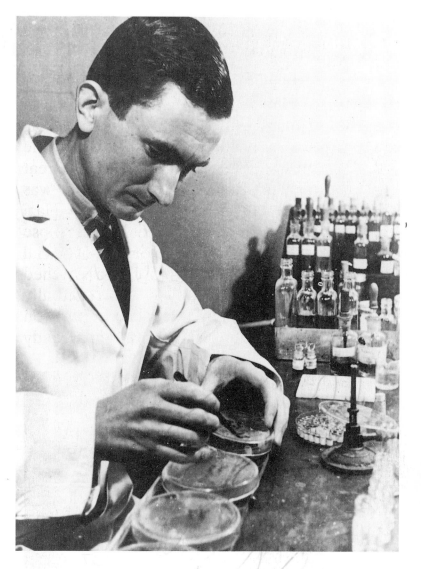

had a sample of Fleming's mould in their culture store. At first, they too found the substance difficult to extract from the culture – it was said to be so unstable that it was lost while you looked at it! Finally, a member of the Florey team, Norman Heatley, came up with an answer, and they managed to produce batches of brown powder from the liquid on which mould grew. In fact, pure penicillin is white. The powder contained only minute amounts of the antibiotic and so they needed to produce a large amount of the powder to be able to carry out experiments to test penicillin's effectiveness on small animals.

The Florey team's penicillin 'factory'. The mould was grown in containers very similar in shape to hospital bedpans.

On 25 May 1940, the team treated four white mice that had been infected with a deadly disease-producing organism, with penicillin. Four other mice that had been infected were not given the penicillin. The following morning, the four treated mice were alive and well, while all four of the untreated mice were dead. Florey, Chain and Heatley were overjoyed. But Florey knew that penicillin had to be tested on humans, and pointed out that 'a man is 3,000 times the size of a mouse'. His team had to find a way of increasing the production of penicillin – he was beginning to realize that it could have an important effect on the outcome of the Second World War, which had broken out eight months earlier.

In August 1940, Florey and Chain published the results of their animal experiments in the medical journal, *The Lancet*. They called their paper, 'Penicillin as a chemotherapeutic agent'. Florey realized that he had to turn his university department into, in effect, a penicillin factory. His team were using all the laboratory flasks and bottles and containers that could be used, but these were not enough. They turned to the nearby hospital for bedpans, which proved to be ideal vessels in which to grow the mould. Heatley then found a company who could supply containers that were shaped like bedpans. By January 1941, they had just enough penicillin to test on humans.

At a nearby hospital there was a policeman who was very sick. He had an infection that had spread to many parts of his body and his doctor did not expect him to survive for long. The policeman received penicillin every day and, by the fourth day, he had dramatically improved. On the fifth day the penicillin began to run out, and gradually his condition became worse and he eventually died. Later, four patients were treated successfully, including a four-year-old child, but once again the supply of penicillin ran out.

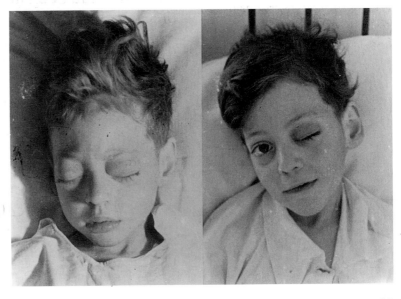

Penicillin cured the infection that threatened the life of this 4-year-old boy. He was the fourth person to be treated with the life-saving medicine.

Florey's team needed to test the drug on a large number of people to prove that it was a safe and effective antibiotic. Unfortunately, the British drug companies, who should have been able to help them, offered little support. It was costly to carry out a major programme of scientific development, and the effectiveness of the drug had not been proven.

The 'miracle' cure that penicillin promised to be, caught the imagination of the press and public in Britain and the USA, encouraged by posters such as this.

Flasks such as these, were first used in the mass-production of penicillin by drug companies.

Florey next looked to the USA, which was not then at war, for help. On 1 July 1941, Florey and Heatley flew to New York, taking precious samples of the mould with them. At the US Department of Agriculture, they were put in touch with Robert Coghill, a man with a lot of experience of growing moulds in large quantities. At his laboratory in Peoria, Illinois, a Dr Moyer found a way of increasing the amount of penicillin that could be extracted from the liquid that the mould grew on.

Then on 7 December 1941, the US naval base at Pearl Harbor, Hawaii, was bombed by Japanese planes. The USA now entered the Second World War, and penicillin production became very important for their war effort. US drug companies like Pfizer, the biggest wartime producer, were asked to help with the production of penicillin. The goal was to produce thousands of kilograms of penicillin.

The drug company, Pfizer, was one of the largest war-time producers of penicillin. Here a man checks the flasks in which the penicillin mould grew.

Florey now returned to Britain to continue his work at Oxford University, while Heatley remained in the USA to observe what was happening there. About this time, Fleming, at St Mary's, asked Florey for some penicillin to treat a friend who was suffering from the serious disease meningitis. The subsequent dramatic cure of his friend was reported by the newspapers, but there was no mention of Fleming. Almoth Wright wanted to set the record straight and he wrote to *The Times* making it clear that it was Fleming who had discovered penicillin. Fleming now became the centre of publicity for the new wonder drug, while Florey and his team at Oxford continued to work quietly in the background.

By 1943, several British drug companies were attempting to mass-produce penicillin and, in that year, Florey travelled to North Africa with just enough of the antibiotic to treat a few soldiers who had received war wounds. The results were impressive. Men who would probably have had to have an arm or a leg amputated because of infection, were cured.

During this time, the original mould discovered by Fleming was being used for the production of penicillin. A new type of penicillin mould was then found on a mouldy melon from a market in Peoria, USA, where Dr Moyer was working. This mould gave more penicillin than Fleming's mould, which meant that penicillin production could be stepped up in time for the D-Day landings. D-Day (6 June 1944) was the first day of the Allied invasion to free Europe from Nazi Germany, and in the hospitals that were set up as the invasion advanced, there was now enough penicillin to treat all the wounded British, American, and other Allied troops.

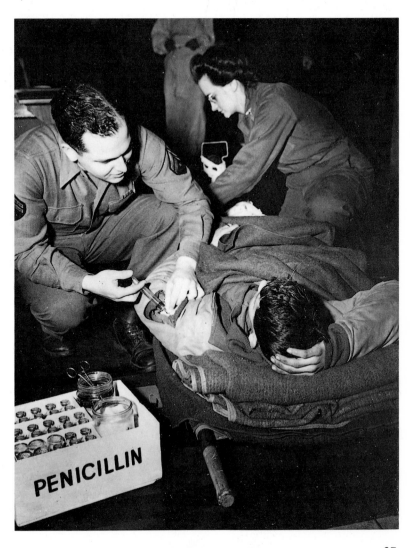

By D-Day (6 June 1944) medical teams had enough penicillin to treat all the Allied troops wounded in battle.

7 A Time of Triumph

A month after D-Day, Fleming and Florey were knighted by King George VI. This was the first of many honours that were to be bestowed on the men who worked on penicillin. Florey was a man of very few words and it was in his nature to be uncompromising. When the newspaper reporters wanted to learn about the part he and his team had played in the development of penicillin, he refused to be interviewed. So it was left to Fleming to be the centre of attention. The unlikely course of events that led to his chance discovery of the mould that gave a 'miracle' cure was an ideal story for the popular press. The reporters would sometimes invent stories about Fleming, which he collected in a special file and delighted in telling to his friends.

(Left to right) *Fleming, Chain and Florey receiving the Nobel Prize for medicine in 1945.*

In 1945, Fleming, Florey and Chain were awarded the Nobel prize for medicine in acknowledgement of their work on penicillin. The prize was the greatest honour possible for the scientists.

In 1946, Fleming was appointed the first director of the Wright-Fleming Institute which was created at St Mary's. The routine jobs that he had formerly carried out were handed to a new, full-time professor. This enabled Fleming to concentrate on the task which he enjoyed – carrying out his own research work.

Fleming was now sixty-five years old and had become an international hero. He travelled to many countries but, as he was a poor public speaker, he failed to excite his audiences and they usually left disappointed. However, the countries he visited were pleased to bestow honours on him. He received many honorary degrees; he was given a special medal by the Pope, and the Legion of Honour by France. In Britain, he was made a Fellow of the Royal Society and a Fellow of the Royal College of Physicians. In 1952, he was installed as Rector of Edinburgh University.

Fleming being carried shoulder-high by students of Edinburgh University after being installed as Rector (chief officer) in 1952.

Fleming receives a presentation gift from the Duke of Edinburgh.

Despite all the honours that were showered on him, Fleming remained a modest, almost shy man. He was often embarrassed at the gifts he received. To overcome his embarrassment, and to thank his admirers, he grew the penicillin mould on small discs of black paper and had them mounted in round glass frames. On the back of them he wrote a message such as: 'The mould that first made penicillin', and signed his name. He gave these in return for the gifts he received from his admirers.

Fleming's presentation gift which he liked to give in return for presents he received.

Fleming and Amalia Coutsouris (his second wife) on their wedding day.

In 1949, Fleming's wife, Sarah, died after an illness. They had been married for thirty-four years and it was a shock from which Fleming was slow to recover. A Greek research assistant, Amalia Voureka Coutsouris, joined the Institute, and as she spoke several languages, she played an important role when important foreign officials visited the Institute. She and Fleming grew fond of one another and in 1953 they married. They lived happily together until Fleming died suddenly of a heart attack on 11 March 1955. He was honoured with a burial in St Paul's Cathedral beside British national heroes and statesmen.

After receiving their Nobel Prizes, Florey and Chain continued to work at Oxford University. In 1960, Florey was elected President of the Royal Society, a very high honour for a man of science, and in 1965, he was made a life peer. He also became Chancellor of the Australian National University and was awarded the Order of Merit.

He died in 1968. In 1949, Chain became a Fellow of the Royal Society. He did not remain at Oxford University – for a number of years he was director of a health institute in Rome, Italy. In 1961, he returned to Britain to take up the post of director of the Wolfson Institute at the Imperial College of Science and Technology, London, where he remained until his retirement in 1973. Chain died in 1979. Another member of the Florey team, Heatley, was awarded Oxford University's first ever Doctorate of Medicine on 20 October 1990. It was the fiftieth anniversary of the successful development of penicillin.

The importance of penicillin in the Allied war effort stimulated further research into antibiotics, and since 1944 there have been many important discoveries. Through the use of antibiotics, medical treatment in the last fifty years has improved dramatically, and, as a result, the average length of life for humans has been enormously increased.

Antibiotics

Antibiotics are chemical substances that are capable of destroying micro-organisms, especially bacteria and fungi. They have revolutionized the treatment of infectious diseases. The word 'antibiosis' was introduced at the end of the nineteenth century to refer to the affect one micro-organism can have on the growth of another micro-organism. It is from this word that 'antibiotic' comes. There are many different antibiotics. Some, like penicillin and cephalosporin, are derived from moulds. Others, like streptomycin and tetracycline, come from bacteria. Some of these can also be made artificially by chemical reaction.

Antibiotics are not effective against viruses. Viruses cause many diseases including influenza, measles, mumps, rabies and AIDS. Vaccines provide immunity to many of these viral diseases.

This picture shows the effect of an antibiotic on harmful bacteria. The ball-shaped bacteria are scattered, with the remains of cells destroyed by the antibiotic weakening the cell walls and causing them to burst.

Norman Heatley (right) photographed with other members of Florey's team on 20 October 1990, when he was awarded Oxford University's first ever Doctorate of Medicine. He received this honour for his role in the development of penicillin. Florey's widow is on the left.

Was Fleming a great scientist? Many people think that he was. He was certainly a very skilled laboratory worker and was very good at envisaging new uses for familiar objects. For example, when testing the sensitivity of bacteria to penicillin, he used a paper punch to make small discs of blotting paper to which he added a precise amount of penicillin. The discs were then placed on the culture plate to see what effect the penicillin would have on the bacteria.

However, Fleming's discovery of penicillin in 1928 was the result of a series of very unlikely events. This is a dramatic example of the part chance plays in many great scientific discoveries. In his own words, 'You've got to be lucky.'

Date Chart

1881 6 August: Alexander Fleming born at Lochfield, Ayrshire, Scotland.

1891 Goes to school at Darvel.

1895 Travels to London and attends the Regent Street Polytechnic.

1897 Becomes a clerk with a shipping company.

1899–1902 The Boer War in South Africa.

1900 Becomes a part-time soldier in the London Scottish Regiment.

1901 Joins Almoth Wright's inoculation department at St Mary's Hospital.

1908 Passes his final medical examinations with honours.

1909 Paul Ehrlich finds a cure for syphilis.

1914 Outbreak of First World War. Serves in France under Wright. Discovers that antiseptics do more harm than good.

1915 Marries Sarah McElroy.

1918 End of First World War. Returns to St Mary's and is appointed lecturer.

1921 Becomes assistant director of the inoculation department.

1922 Discovers lysozyme.

1928 Discovers penicillin; made professor of bacteriology.

1929 Publishes his findings on penicillin.

1930–32 Harold Raistrick and his team fail to purify penicillin.

1935 Sulphonamide drugs discovered.

1939 Outbreak of Second World War.

1940 Florey and Chain solve the problem of extracting penicillin; they publish the results of animal experiments.

1941 First human patient tested with penicillin; Florey and Heatley fly to the USA hoping to interest the Americans in penicillin.

1943 British drug companies attempt to mass-produce penicillin.

1944 Penicillin used during D-Day invasion; Fleming and Florey knighted.

1945 End of Second World War; Fleming, Florey and Chain receive Nobel prize for medicine.

1946 Becomes director of Wright-Fleming Institute.

1949 Death of wife, Sarah.

1953 Marries Amalia Coutsouris.

1955 11 March: dies of a heart attack.

Glossary

Abscess A collection of pus.

Antibiotic A substance such as penicillin that kills micro-organisms.

Antiseptics Chemicals that can kill micro-organisms.

Bacteria Tiny single-celled organisms. Some bacteria cause disease.

Bacteriologist Someone who studies bacteria.

Biochemist Someone who studies the reaction of chemical compounds occurring in living organisms.

Cultures Bacteria that have been grown in special dishes called Petri dishes, so that they can be examined.

Fungus A type of plant that lacks leaves, true stems and roots. It spreads and reproduces by air-borne spores.

Germ A micro-organism, especially one that produces disease.

Immune Protected against an infection.

Immunization To make a person immune by inoculation.

Infection Invasion of the body by harmful organisms.

Inoculation The introduction of a vaccine in order to make a person immune to a disease.

Micro-organism Any organism too small to see with the naked eye.

Mould A type of fungus.

Organisms Living plants and animals, including bacteria, viruses and fungi.

Paper A formal essay on a subject.

Syphilis A disease transmitted by sexual intercourse.

Tetanus An acute infectious disease causing convulsions.

Vaccine Any infection employed to produce immunity to a particular disease.

Virus An ultra-small organism that can only be seen with a powerful electron microscope. Viruses are the cause of many diseases.

Books to Read

Alexander Fleming by Josephine Ross (Hamish Hamilton, 1981)

Alexander Fleming: the Man and the Myth by Gwyn Macfarlane (Chatto & Windus, 1984)

Sir Alexander Fleming: Man of Penicillin by John Malken (Alloway Publishing, 1981)

Alexander Fleming by Richard Tames (Franklin Watts, 1990)

Health and Medicine by Brenda Walpole (Wayland, 1991)

Picture acknowledgements

Mary Evans 5, 16, 17; Imperial War Museum 20, 21, 37; Kilmarnock and Loudon District Museum 8; Norman McBeath 45; Pfizer Drug Company 36; Popperfoto cover, iii, 24, 35, 39, 41; St Mary's Hospital 4, 9, 10, 11, 12, 13, 14, 15, 18, 23, 25, 26, 34, 38, 40; St Mary's Hospital/Science Picture Library 29, 42; Science Picture Library 6, 19, 22, 27, 28; Sir William Dunn School of Pathology 7, 30, 31, 32, 33, 43. Cover artwork is by Richard Hook.

Index